HEINEMANN STATE STUDIES

Illinois
Plants and Animals

Andrew Santella

Heinemann Librar
Chicago, Illinois

© 2003 Reed Educational & Professional Publishing
Published by Heinemann Library,
an imprint of Reed Educational & Professional
Publishing, Chicago, Illinois

Customer Service 888-454-2279

Visit our website at www.heinemannlibrary.com

Designed by Heinemann Library
Page layout by Depke Design
Printed and bound in the United States by Lake
Book Manufacturing, Inc.

07 06 05 04 03
10 9 8 7 6 5 4 3 2 1

**Library of Congress
Cataloging-in-Publication Data**
Santella, Andrew.
   Illinois plants and animals / by Andrew Santella.
      v. cm. -- (State studies)
Includes bibliographical references (p. 47).
Contents: Wild illinois -- Plants and animals at risk -
- Where they live -- Illinois's plants and animals --
Then and now.
   ISBN 1-40340-011-3 (HC), 1-40340-572-7 (Pbk)
   1. Zoology--Illinois--Juvenile literature. 2. Botany--
Illinois--Juvenile literature. [1. Zoology--Illinois.
2. Botany--Illinois.] I. Title. II. State studies
(Heinemann Library (Firm))
   QH105.I3 S26 2002
   578'.09773--dc21
                              2002000798

Acknowledgments
The author and publishers are grateful to the
following for permission to reproduce copyright
material:

Cover photographs by (TL-TR): Robert Lifson/
Heinemann Library; Jeremy Woodhouse/PhotoDisc;
Robert Lifson/Heinemann Library; James P. Rowan;
(bottom) Susan Day/Daybreak Imagery

pp. 4, 22, 27, 29, 31, 34, 35 Richard Day/
Daybreak Imagery; pp. 5, 17, 42 maps.com/
Heinemann Library; pp. 6, 7, 13, 20, 30, 33, 34,
36, 40, 41, 43 James P. Rowan; p. 8 Illinois
Department of Commerce and Community Affairs;
pp. 9, 18, 21, 26 Robert Lifson/Heinemann Library;
p. 10 The Granger Collection, NY; p. 11 Visuals
Unlimited; p. 12 Kennan Ward/Corbis; p. 14T
Layne Kennedy/Corbis; p. 14B Illinois State
Museum/Gary Androshko; p. 15 Bettmann/ Corbis;
p. 16 Will Troyer/Visuals Unlimited; p. 19 The
Samuel Roberts Noble Foundation, Inc.; p. 23 Milt
Mann/Cameramann International; p. 24 U.S. Army
Corps of Engineers; p. 25 Corbis; p. 28 David G.
Campbell/Visuals Unlimited; p. 32 Susan Day/
Daybreak Imagery; p. 36 Ohio Department of
Natural Resources; pp. 37, 44 Courtesy of
Fermilab; p. 38 Rob & Ann Simpson/Visuals
Unlimited; p. 39 Beth Davidow/Visuals Unlimited;
p. 45 Stephen J. Krasemann/Photo Researchers

Special thanks to Tom Schwartz of the Illinois
Historic Preservation Agency, for his expert help
and advice on the series.

Every effort has been made to contact copyright
holders of any material reproduced in this book.
Any omissions will be rectified in subsequent
printings if notice is given to the publisher.

Some words are shown in bold, **like this.**
You can find out what they mean by looking
in the glossary.

Contents

Wild Illinois

Illinois is lucky enough to have many kinds of plant and animal life. Bald eagles soar over the Mississippi River, searching for fish to eat. Bobcats climb trees in the forests of southern Illinois to spot **prey** such as mice and squirrels. Monarch butterflies fly 2,000 miles (3,200 kilometers) from Mexico to return to their summer homes in Illinois each year. In the forests of northwest Illinois, bur oak trees grow 120 feet (36.5 meters) tall and may live for 1,000 years. Beneath their branches, newborn **fawns** take their first steps in the spring. At night, hundreds of tiger salamanders come out from hiding places beneath logs searching for mice and worms to eat. In small patches of Illinois prairie, thousands of wildflowers of nearly every color bloom.

Monarch butterflies (left) return from Mexico to Illinois each spring, flying thousands of miles. Bald eagles (below) can be found along the Mississippi River.

Illinois

Galena
Rockford
Byron
Elgin
Dixon
Tampico
Rock Island
Moline
La Salle
Bishop Hill
Galesburg
Peoria
Eureka
Pekin
Normal
Bloomington
Nauvoo
Champaign
Danville
Urbana
Quincy
New Salem
Springfield
Arthur
Lake Shelbyville
Mattoon
Effingham
Godfrey
Vandalia
Alton
Edwardsville
Carlyle Lake
East St. Louis
Cahokia
Centralia
Mt. Vernon
Grayville
Prairie du Rocher
Rend Lake
Kaskaskia
Shawneetown
Carbondale
Cairo

Waukegan
Arlington Heights
Des Plaines
Evanston
Skokie
Oak Park
Chicago
Wheaton
Aurora
Naperville
Joliet
Illinois & Michigan Canal
Kankakee

Mississippi River
Fox River
Rock River
Illinois River
Kankakee River
Sangamon River
Kaskaskia River
Embarras River
Wabash River
Big Muddy River
Ohio River

N
W E
S

0   50 mi.
0   50 km

Thousands of **species** of plants and animals live in Illinois. A species is a group of living things that resemble one another, have common **ancestors,** and can breed with one another. There are about 3,000 species of plants and 30,000 species of animals in Illinois. Illinois is home to about 500 types of trees and shrubs. It also has nearly 2,000 kinds of flowering plants. Illinois can claim 300 kinds of birds, 200 species of fish, and 60

Illinois Beach State Park stretches along 6.5 miles (10.5 kilometers) of the Lake Michigan shoreline. Sandy dunes in the park (above) are home to more than 650 species of plants.

species of mammals. In Illinois, you can also find 46 kinds of snakes, 19 kinds of salamanders, and 21 types of frogs and toads.

MAKING HOMES FOR LIVING THINGS

Why do so many different kinds of plants and animals live in Illinois? Its **climate** and the shape of the land itself make Illinois an attractive home for so many kinds of plants and animals. From north to south, Illinois is one of the longest states in the country. It is 385 miles (620 kilometers) long from its northern border to the Ohio River in the south. In between, plants and animals can find homes in many types of climates. Plants and animals that flourish in cool conditions can find a home in northern Illinois. Plants and animals that do well in warmer conditions can find a home in southern Illinois.

Moisture conditions vary across the state, as well. The shoreline of Lake Michigan is more wet and humid than the dry plains of central Illinois. In southern Illinois, bald cypress trees grow in standing water in swamps. Differences in moisture across Illinois make it possible for the state to support many kinds of plants and animals.

There are many different kinds of soil conditions found across Illinois, too. In Illinois, you can visit swamps, forests, river bluffs, canyons, and sandy beaches. All these different kinds of land and soil offer shelter to different kinds of plants and animals.

Fifty thousand years ago, **glaciers** covered much of Illinois. Glaciers are huge sheets of ice that move slowly across land. The last glaciers retreated from Illinois about 12,000 years ago, due to a change in climate. When they melted away, they left behind **minerals** that

A visitor enjoys the view from a rock outcropping at Garden of the Gods (left), which is located in the Shawnee National Forest at the southern tip of Illinois. The Shawnee National Forest is the only national forest in Illinois. It is home to 253 species of birds alone.

made the soil of central Illinois some of the richest in the world. The same **glaciers** shaped other parts of the state, as well. Near Chicago, they carved out shallow lakes and ponds. Some parts of Illinois were never covered by glaciers. As a result, that land was never flattened by a glacier's powerful movements. Parts of southern Illinois and northwestern Illinois are therefore very hilly.

According to the Illinois Department of Natural Resources, Illinois has 90 different **habitats.** A habitat is a home in nature for plants and animals. Beavers, fish, turtles, and **waterfowl** make homes in rivers. Songbirds and squirrels live among trees in forests and cities. Game birds and rabbits find homes in farm fields. In **bogs,** trees and shrubs grow on floating mats of moss.

PLANT AND ANIMAL LIFE AROUND US

Plant and animal life can be found everywhere in Illinois. Wildflowers bloom along highways. Tall grasses grow in small patches of prairie along railroad tracks. Red-winged blackbirds perch on **reeds** in wet **marshes.** The ledges of city **skyscrapers** provide a home for rock doves, which are also called pigeons.

Illinois plants and animals live in forests, **swamps,** rivers, lakes, prairies, farm fields, and cities. Nature preserves and wildlife **refuges** provide homes for many **species,** too. People flock to state parks to see wild-flowers each spring.

The plants and animals of Illinois are natural **resources.** A natural resource is something found in nature that people value. Knowing more about Illinois's plants and animals helps us to preserve and protect them. Without our care, some of these plants and animals could vanish from Illinois forever.

Wildflowers (right and below) bloom even along highways and railroads in Illinois. They can be found in every part of the state in many different shapes and colors.

Plants and Animals at Risk

Illinois became a state in 1818. That year, only about 35,000 people lived in Illinois. That's about as many people as live in a medium-sized city or **suburb** today. There was one animal that greatly outnumbered people in Illinois. That animal was the passenger pigeon. Millions of passenger pigeons lived in Illinois and nearby states. They lived on fruits and nuts that they gathered from trees. Sometimes, so many passenger pigeons perched on a single tree branch that the branch would snap under the weight of the birds. Flying from one place to another, huge flocks of passenger pigeons would darken the sky.

Less than 100 years later, passenger pigeons had vanished from Illinois and the rest of the world. What happened to these birds? They were killed off by hunters. Settlers in Illinois had always hunted passenger pigeons. However, around 1840, hunters began killing greater numbers of the birds. Pigeons had become a favorite treat of diners in big

In the early 1800s, so many passenger pigeons (left) flew overhead that they could sometimes block out sunlight for hours.

cities around the world. Hunters learned they could make money by killing pigeons and sending the meat to other cities in refrigerated railroad cars. They hunted pigeons with guns and gathered young pigeons from nests. These young pigeons were considered the most delicious of all. They were also the easiest to capture. Soon there were not enough young passenger pigeons to replace older pigeons that were being killed. By 1900, only a few passenger pigeons still lived in the wild. In 1914, the last passenger pigeon died in a zoo in Cincinnati, Ohio. In less than 100 years, a huge population had been wiped out.

VANISHING SPECIES

Passenger pigeons are called an **extinct species.** An extinct species is one that no longer survives anywhere in the world. Passenger pigeons are not the only extinct species that once lived in Illinois. Another kind of bird called the Carolina parakeet once lived among fruit trees in southern Illinois. The Carolina parakeets were killed off by hunters who gathered their feathers for hats. Fruit growers also considered Carolina parakeets

Saber-toothed cats (left) are an extinct species of Illinois. Their canine teeth were shaped like sabers (curved swords) and were eight inches (20 centimeters) long. Saber-toothed cats hunted thick-skinned animals like the **mastodon.**

The peregrine falcon (above) is an endangered species of Illinois. Peregrines hunt birds by knocking them from the sky. They usually prefer to hunt small birds.

pests because they ate up the fruit of their orchards. Now the Carolina parakeet is **extinct.** Six kinds of mussels that once lived in Illinois rivers are also extinct. A mussel is a shelled animal that lives in water. Pollution in rivers helped kill them off. Some animals that lived in Illinois thousands of years ago are extinct, too. These include the **mammoth,** the **mastodon,** and the **saber-toothed cats.**

Some **species** no longer live in Illinois but continue to live in other places. These are called **extirpated** species. Herds containing hundreds of **bison** once roamed Illinois. Hunting by settlers killed off all the bison in Illinois by 1830. However, they continued to live in other places. They were extirpated from Illinois. Black bears, elk, and porcupines have also been extirpated from Illinois. Today, bison have actually been reintroduced in protected areas in Illinois.

An **endangered** species is one that is in danger of extinction. The peregrine falcon is an endangered species of Illinois. It is the fastest animal in the world. Peregrine falcons are capable of diving at 200 miles per hour (322 kilometers per hour) when trying to catch mice or other **prey.** However, they were nearly wiped out in the 1960s by a dangerous chemical used in farming called DDT. They also suffered when many of the large, hollow trees they nest in were cut down. Today, falcons have learned to find new homes in city **skyscrapers.** However, the falcon remains an endangered animal. Many plants in Illinois are endangered, as well. They include grasses like

blue grama and flowering plants like the wild hyacinth.

A **threatened** species is one that could become endangered soon. The timber rattlesnake lives in southern Illinois forests. Because of hunting and the clearing of their forest homes, fewer of these snakes are living in Illinois. They are a threatened species. River otters and sandhill cranes are other examples of threatened animals. The tamarack tree and the brightly flowered blazing star plant are examples of threatened plants.

The blazing star (above) is a tall, thin plant from 1 to 6 feet (30 to 180 centimeters) high that is found in Illinois. Thick clusters of small purple blossoms grow along the stem on thin spikes.

LIFE FROM LONG AGO

Some extinct animals lived in Illinois millions of years ago. Trilobites are extinct animals that were related to

Endangered and Threatened Species

The Illinois Endangered Species Protection Act (IESPA) was put into effect in 1973. Its goal is to protect Illinois's rare native species of plants and animals. According to the Illinois Endangered Species Protection Board, there are 147 animals and 331 plants on the list of endangered and threatened species in Illinois. These are the mammals on that list:

Endangered mammals:		Threatened mammals:
eastern big-eared bat	Indiana bat	river otter
southeastern bat	eastern woodrat	golden mouse
gray bat		marsh rice rat

Fossil remains tell us that 500 million years ago, trilobites (above) swam in the seas of Illinois and crawled on the muddy sea floors.

today's crabs and lobsters. They lived 500 million years ago, when Illinois was covered by warm, shallow seas. Most trilobites were only about 2 inches (5 centimeters) long, but some grew as large as 2 feet (61 centimeters) long. They had shells like crabs, which survive as **fossils.** Fossils are the remains of plants or animals that lived long ago.

Illinois's state fossil is the Tully monster. The Tully monster was a sea animal with a soft body and fins for swimming. It lived in the seas and **swamps** that covered Illinois 300 million years ago.

No fossil remains of dinosaurs have been found in Illinois yet. However, it is possible that some lived in Illinois. Hadrosaurs, which are duck-billed dinosaurs, lived in nearby Missouri 65 million years ago. Hadrosaurs were plant-eating dinosaurs with flat bills similar to that of a modern duck. They had larger brains than most other plant-eating dinosaurs.

*The Tully monster (below) swam in Illinois waters 300 million years ago. It fed on shrimp and jellyfish, two **species** that still exist today.*

MAMMOTHS, MASTODONS, AND SABER-TOOTHED CATS

Fifteen thousand years ago, Illinois had a much cooler **climate** than it does today. As a result, plants that do well in cool temperatures lived in Illinois at that time. For example, spruce and poplar trees grew

there. Today, those trees are found in cooler places, like Minnesota, and high in the Rocky Mountains.

Besides tusks, mastodons (above) also had teeth that were 3 inches (7.5 centimeters) wide and 6 inches (15 centimeters) long, which they used to grind the plants they ate.

Mastodons and **mammoths** fed on the plants of Illinois. Mammoths grew to about 13 feet (4 meters) tall and weighed about 8 tons (7.3 metric tons). They ate plants in grassy areas. Mastodons were smaller. They grew to about 10 feet (3 meters) tall and weighed 6 tons (5.4 metric tons). They lived in forests.

At about the same time, **saber-toothed cats** roamed Illinois. Saber-toothed cats were named for their large, sharp upper teeth. They may have used these teeth to kill the large animals that they hunted. They may also have used them to scare other animals, just as modern animals use their antlers and horns.

About 11,000 years ago, Illinois slowly became warmer. Plant life became more like today's plant life. The warmer temperatures drove some animals out of Illinois. Human hunters killed off large numbers of other animals. Mastodons, mammoths, and saber-toothed cats had all vanished from Illinois by 9000 B.C.E.

Where They Live

All plants and animals need the same basic things to survive. They need food, water, shelter, and space. They find these things in their **habitats,** or homes. If any of those things are missing, they may not survive.

Plants and animals also need other plants and animals to survive. A community of living things that depend on each other and on their natural surroundings is called an **ecosystem.** In an ecosystem, each living thing depends on other living things for its survival. If one **species** fails to survive, other members of the system may also suffer.

There are many kinds of ecosystems in Illinois. Some are natural, which means humans did not help create them. Others are human-made. The major natural ecosystems of Illinois are prairies, woodlands, **wetlands,** lakes, and rivers. Each of these systems

A beaver's thick fur keeps it warm, even when it is wet. That's one of several adaptations that help it survive in Illinois wetlands.

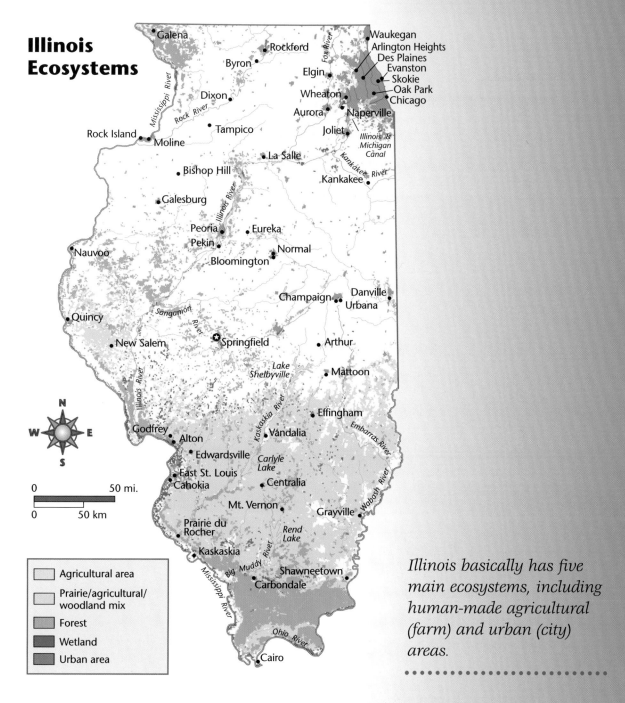

Illinois Ecosystems

Galena
Rockford
Waukegan
Arlington Heights
Byron
Des Plaines
Elgin
Evanston
Skokie
Wheaton
Oak Park
Dixon
Chicago
Aurora
Naperville
Rock Island
Tampico
Joliet
Moline
Illinois & Michigan Canal
La Salle
Kankakee River
Bishop Hill
Kankakee
Galesburg
Peoria
Eureka
Pekin
Normal
Nauvoo
Bloomington
Champaign
Danville
Urbana
Quincy
New Salem
Springfield
Arthur
Lake Shelbyville
Mattoon
Sangamon River
Effingham
Godfrey
Vandalia
Embarras River
Alton
Edwardsville
Carlyle Lake
East St. Louis
Cahokia
Centralia
Mt. Vernon
Grayville
Prairie du Rocher
Rend Lake
Kaskaskia
Shawneetown
Carbondale
Cairo
Ohio River
Big Muddy River
Wabash River
Kaskaskia River
Mississippi River
Rock River
Illinois River
Fox River

Legend:
- Agricultural area
- Prairie/agricultural/woodland mix
- Forest
- Wetland
- Urban area

Scale: 0 — 50 mi. / 0 — 50 km

Illinois basically has five main ecosystems, including human-made agricultural (farm) and urban (city) areas.

includes many other, smaller systems. The major human-made ecosystems are farms and cities (or agricultural and **urban**).

Plants and animals develop **adaptations** that make them well-suited to their homes. An adaptation is a feature of a plant or animal that helps it survive in a certain habitat or ecosystem. For example, beavers have several adaptations that help them live in rivers and ponds. Their thick, waterproof fur keeps them warm even when they are wet.

Their webbed back feet act like paddles that help them swim. Their teeth are sharp enough to cut down small trees, which they use to make their homes.

PRAIRIES

Illinois is called the Prairie State because much of it was once covered by flat grasslands called prairies. When settlers arrived in Illinois in the early 1800s, they found vast stretches of prairie. In some places they could see endless fields of grasses and flowers. They told stories of grass so tall that it covered a man on horseback. Before 1800, more than half of Illinois was covered by prairie, including almost all of the central and northern regions.

Where Are the Trees?

Very few trees grow in prairie **habitats.** Settlers in the 1800s could stand in one spot on an Illinois prairie and look in all directions without seeing a single tree. Scientists are still debating why trees don't grow on prairies. It may be because certain kinds of **climates** make it easier for grasses to grow than trees. For example, prairie grasses may  have an easier time surviving in very dry conditions and high winds than would trees. Also, the kind of soil found in prairies may be better-suited to grasses over trees. Finally, fires keep trees from taking root in prairies. Native Americans used to set fire to prairies to hunt buffalo. Lightning often started fires on dry prairies, too. These fires would burn any plant life above the ground. Unlike trees, most prairie plants have deep roots that can survive a fire. The parts above ground burn, but their roots stay alive and sprout again.

The first settlers in Illinois avoided the prairies. They had never seen anything like them before. Trees were scarce in prairies, and farmers needed wood for fuel and building material. However, settlers soon found that prairie soil was very **fertile.** It would make fine farmland. And since there were no trees to cut down, all Illinois farmers needed was a plow that would work in prairie soil. Prairie plants like red root, also known as New Jersey tea, sent tough roots deep into the ground. These roots made plowing nearly impossible. Then, in 1837, an Illinois blacksmith named John Deere provided a solution. He invented a steel plow that could cut cleanly through roots. Deere's steel plow was so smooth that soil did not stick to it.

Red root plants (above) send roots deep into Illinois soil, which helps them survive extreme weather and prairie fires. It took John Deere's plow to defeat plants like this.

John Deere's plow made it possible to turn the prairie into farmland. By 1900, most of Illinois's prairie had vanished. In its place stood farms. In the 1900s, growing cities and **suburbs** replaced other bits of prairie. About 22 million acres (8.9 million hectares) of prairie once covered Illinois. Today, only about 2,500 acres (1,000 hectares) survive. Prairie can be found in out-of-the-way places like near old railroad tracks and in closed cemeteries.

Large animals that once lived in Illinois prairies could not exist in the small spaces of prairie that were left. **Bison,** black bears, and other animals had to find new homes. So did many **species** of birds, insects, and plants. However, Illinois prairies are still home to hundreds of

Burning Prairies

Prairies are mostly flat and often very dry. They are a perfect place for fires to spread. Native Americans set fires to trap **bison** during their hunts. They would surround a herd of bison and set a fire that almost formed a circle around the herd. The fire would drive the bison to a place where Native American hunters were waiting with bows and arrows. A French **missionary** named Louis Hennepin described the Miami people using fire to hunt bison near Kankakee in 1679: "When they see a herd they gather in great numbers and set fire to the grass everywhere around these animals, except some passage which they leave on purpose and where they take post with their bows and arrows. The bison, seeking to escape the fire are thus compelled to pass near these Indians, who sometimes kill as many as a hundred and twenty in a day." Some prairie fires could burn out of control. The only thing that could stop such a fire was a large river. One fire, in 1836, may have been caused by lightning or set by a local farmer. It spread rapidly and burned for 60 miles (96.5 kilometers). It started near the Spoon River in Stark County and didn't stop until it reached the Rock River near Rockford.

kinds of plants and animals. Some of them can only survive in prairies. Their future depends on preserving prairie **habitats.**

WOODLANDS

Before 1800, nearly half of Illinois was covered by trees and shrubs. The southern tip was almost all forest. In other parts of the state, trees and shrubs grew in different kinds of woodlands. On the edge of a prairie, a single oak tree might stand alone with no other trees nearby. Other trees grew in **groves,** or small groups of trees. Dense forests also contained shrubs, **herbs,** grasses, and ferns.

In the 1800s, settlers cleared much of Illinois's woodlands to make room for farms. They cut down trees and burned out their roots and stumps. Sometimes they killed a tree by cutting away its bark in a ring around its trunk. This was called **girdling.**

Today, only a small portion of Illinois's original woodlands remain. However, they are growing again. Land once used for grazing farm animals is again becoming covered with new trees and shrubs. These new forests are called second-growth forests. They exist mostly in scattered places around the state.

Lack of space makes it difficult for some plant and animal **species** to survive. The invasion of species from outside Illinois also harms native plants and animals. This makes woodlands even more important homes for Illinois wildlife. Most species of mammals and birds need to spend at least some of their time in forests to survive.

The Shawnee National Forest (left) in southern Illinois contains some of the state's original woodlands. It is an important habitat, since many plants and animals need the woods to survive.

WETLANDS

Wetlands are areas of very wet, low-lying land. Some wetlands are covered with water all the time. Other wetlands are not covered with water, but have very damp, soggy soil. In the 1800s, Illinois settlers thought wetlands were worthless. In fact, they thought many diseases came from wetlands. They dug drainage ditches to carry water away from wetlands. Then they covered them with dry soil. In this way, much of Illinois's wetlands were turned into farms or **suburban** neighborhoods. In 1800, there were about 9 million acres (3.5 million hectares) of wetlands in the state. Today, about 500,000 acres (200,000 hectares) survive. This loss of **habitat** has made it difficult for hundreds of kinds of wetland plants and animals to survive.

However, wetlands continue to be important in Illinois. They act as **filters** that trap **sediments** that would otherwise pollute rivers and lakes. They also act as sponges that take in water from rainfall and melting snow. This helps prevent flooding. Wetlands are also home to some of Illinois's most remarkable plants and animals. Millions of **waterfowl** pass through wetlands during their spring and fall **migrations.** Wetlands are also home to hundreds of kinds of insects, mammals, amphibians, and reptiles.

Male (left) and female (right) mallards make their home in Illinois wetlands. These birds tip bottom-up in shallow water, stretching their necks to feed on the bottom. They take off from water in quick jumps when they fly.

RIVERS

Illinois rivers have always been important to human settlements. Native Americans lived along rivers and streams. So did the white settlers in the 1800s. More than 30,000 miles (48,000 kilometers) of rivers and streams flow through Illinois. Their waters are home to fish, insects, **aquatic** plants, and mammals. In the late 1800s and early 1900s, some of Illinois's rivers became badly polluted. Factories and **stockyards** dumped their waste into rivers. Sediments from farm fields washed into rivers. They block the light that aquatic plants need to survive. As a result, native plants and animals suffer.

Human actions affected rivers in other ways, as well. Throughout Illinois history, people built **dams** on some rivers. They **dredged** others to make them deeper, so larger boats could travel on them. These actions changed the habitat upon which the plants and animals depended. Native plants and animals also had to compete with new **species** from other places. Many of the new species were better able to survive the effects of pollution.

This statue is located in Allen Park on the Illinois River in Ottawa. The buildings and bridge in the background show how man has changed nature.

In the last 20 years, Illinois rivers have become cleaner. As a result, they make better homes for animals and plants. For example, the number of native minnows and green sunfish in the upper Illinois River have greatly increased.

LAKES

It may not be easy to see from shore, but thousands of plants and animals live beneath the surface of Illinois lakes. Lake shores and beaches are important habitats, too. One of the world's largest lakes makes up Illinois's northeast border. Lake Michigan supports many kinds of animal and plant life. It also provides more than one million gallons (3.7 million liters) of drinking water for Chicago and its **suburbs** each year.

Lake Shelbyville (right) was created by damming a river. The lake was created to reduce flooding and provide water during dry periods. Changing nature like this can create new habitats, but it can also destroy the original habitats.

Illinois is also home to smaller lakes. Some of these are human-made. For example, Lake Shelbyville and Carlyle Lake (see map on page 17) were made in the 1960s by **damming** rivers. They were created to reduce flooding and provide water during dry periods. Turning rivers into lakes creates new habitats for animals. However, it also destroys habitats that already existed.

Human actions have affected plants and animals in lakes. People took so many fish from Lake Michigan in the late 1800s and early 1900s that some native **species,** such as lake trout, nearly died out. People also brought in new species that competed with native species and sometimes drove them out.

The quality of the water in Illinois lakes is harmed by pollution. Chemicals from farm soil are washed into lakes from rivers. This reduces the amount of oxygen in water. Plants and fish need oxygen to survive. **Sediments** from rivers sometimes wash into lakes. This takes up space and reduces the amount of water in the lakes. Only if people protect the quality of water in lakes will plants and animals continue to find a home there.

CITIES, SUBURBS, AND FARMS

We don't think of cities as places to find nature. However, city neighborhoods form an **ecosystem.** So do office parks, backyards, and farms. These are all human-made ecosystems. They were built where natural ecosystems once existed. For example, parts of Chicago were built on **marshes.** The species that lived there had to find other **habitats.** They were replaced by species that could survive in the city.

Farms replaced prairies in much of Illinois. Some prairie species were able to survive on farmland. Those species learned to survive in the fields of hay and **pastures** used to graze, or feed, farm animals. However, neither hay fields nor livestock pastures are as common as they used to be in Illinois. As a result, species that found shelter there have had to find new homes once again.

Human-made ecosystems such as cities support plant and animal life, too. Peregrine falcons have learned to live on Chicago (below) skyscrapers and hunt pigeons.

Plants and Animals

There is not a single place in Illinois that does not support a large variety of plant and animal life. The prairie is still one of Illinois's several **ecosystems.** It supports many kinds of plants and animals.

PRAIRIE LIFE

The main plant in prairies is grass. However, prairie grass is different from the grass that makes up lawns. The biggest difference is in the roots. Prairie grasses have much longer roots than lawn grass. Most of Illinois's prairies are tallgrass prairies. They are made up mostly of tough grasses like switchgrass and big bluestem. Big bluestem is the state prairie grass of Illinois. Its roots go as deep as 7 feet (2.1 meters) underground. Switchgrass roots may be 11 feet (3.4 meters)

Grasses grow tall on the Illinois prairie. They depend on root systems that go deep beneath the surface.

Upland Sandpiper

Some prairie birds **migrate** to warmer places in the winter. The prize for longest distance traveled each year goes to the upland sandpiper (left). These birds fly all the way to Argentina, in South America, for the winter. This is a distance of about 5,000 miles (8,050 kilometers).

The upland sandpiper is known for its long, loud whistle. It uses its long beak to pick grasshoppers, crickets, beetles, and moths off plants. If it can't find insects, it will eat seeds. Hunters in the late 1800s killed many upland sandpipers in Illinois. They suffered from the loss of prairie **habitat,** as well. Some have found new homes in farm fields or even in open spaces like airports. One of the best places to see upland sandpipers is at Midewin National Tallgrass Prairie in Will County, Illinois.

long. These grasses grow several feet tall and bend and wave in the wind.

Mixed in with the grasses in prairies are wildflowers of many colors, like goldenrod and coneflowers. In all, more than 800 types of plants are native to Illinois prairies. From April to October, something is almost always in bloom on a prairie. In spring, violets produce bright purple flowers. In the fall, some asters are still blooming gold and purple. Prairie plants live beneath the ground, too. Some prairie plants send roots as far as 20 feet (6 meters) below ground. These plants can live for decades. When they die, their root systems **decay** and make the soil rich. This helps other plants grow in their place.

The grasses and flowers of the prairie attract and support many kinds of birds and insects. Butterflies find nectar in prairie flowers. When they are in their caterpillar stage, they feed on grasses. Dogbane leaf beetles feed on plants such as milkweed and dogbane. To drive away **predators,** they sometimes give off a foul-smelling odor when they are touched.

Only some types of birds can survive on prairies. Since there are few trees, some prairie birds have to be able to perch on stems of prairie grass and build their nests on the ground. Birds such as the bobolink even learn to sing while they are flying, since there are often no tree branches to perch on. Birds like the meadowlark hunt insects such as caterpillars, beetles, and grasshoppers. They eat seeds and grain in winter. Owls use their sharp eyesight to hunt for mice at night.

The smooth green snake is one of the most common of all snakes found in prairies. It is a non-venomous (not poisonous) snake that measures only about 15 inches (38 centimeters) long. Smooth green snakes feed on crickets and grasshoppers. They may be spotted crossing bike trails, but they're hard to see in grass. That's because of their bright green color. In the winter, prairie snakes dig a hole underground to keep warm until spring.

Smooth green snakes (below) are hard to spot in green grass. That is what protects them. They are not poisonous and are only about 15 inches (38 centimeters) long.

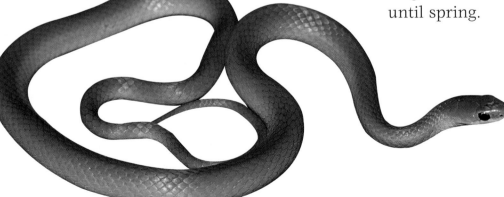

Badgers (right) use their strong front legs to dig through the roots of prairie grasses. Badgers are expert diggers, especially for their size. They dig complicated underground tunnels in which they live. If they cannot escape an enemy, badgers become savage fighters. They use their claws and teeth as weapons and are protected by their thick fur and tough skin.

Some animals have special **adaptations** to help them live in the prairie. Badgers have very strong front legs that allow them to dig through tough prairie grass roots. When they sense danger, they hide underground. Woodchucks hunt for insects and other small animals underground. They use their strong sense of smell to help them find food in the dark. Plants use adaptations, too. Grasses send their roots deep under the surface to find moisture during long dry spells. Wildflowers bloom in bright colors to attract bees and wasps. The bees and wasps help spread flowering plants to other parts of the prairie.

FOREST LIFE

Illinois's forests were very important to the settlers who moved there in the early 1800s. Native hickory trees provided wood for fuel. Sugar maples supplied sap that could be made into maple syrup. The wood of the white oak was used to make furniture and fences.

Those settlers cleared most of the state's forests. Today, forests are coming back in some protected parts of Illinois. Sand Ridge State Forest near Peoria is Illinois's largest state forest. It offers more than 7,500 acres (3,000 hectares) of oak and hickory trees, much like the ones the first settlers found.

Of course, forests are much more than trees. Wildflowers grow along the ground. Hepatica is one of the most common forest wildflowers and has white, pink, and blue flowers. Nodding trillium can be found in moist woods. Its flowers hang on a long stem beneath its leaves.

One of the first things a person notices when entering a forest is the singing of birds. Some birds make other sounds, too. Woodpeckers drum away at tree trunks with their long bills, searching for insects. The woodpecker's beak is an **adaptation** to the forest that allows it to peck into wood and scoop insects out. Cooper's hawks soar overhead looking for small birds to eat. American kestrels use their sharp eyesight to spot grasshoppers up to 100 feet (30 meters) away.

Hepatica (below) grows wild in Illinois forests, as do many other flowers. There is much more than trees in a forest ecosystem.

On the floors of forests, squirrels gather nuts and search for places to hide them. Some

Opossums

The opossum (left) is the only marsupial in North America. Marsupials are animals that grow up in a pouch on their mother's stomach. Marsupials also have more teeth than any other North American mammal—50. Opossums use their tails to hang from tree branches. When cornered, an opossum will sometimes play dead. Because of this, playing dead is sometimes called "playing 'possum." However, when faced with danger, opossums may also hiss, growl, and show their teeth.

squirrels can hide about 25 nuts in one half hour. Salamanders hide themselves under logs and in other dark places in forests. At night, they come out to search for worms to eat. The largest land salamander in Illinois is the tiger salamander, which can be up to 13 inches (33 centimeters) long. It is named for its dark body and yellow spots, which make it look like a tiger.

WETLAND LIFE

French fur traders were among the first Europeans to visit Illinois. They came here in the late 1600s looking for an animal that lived in **wetlands:** the beaver. Native Americans had long trapped and hunted beavers for their long, thick fur. In the 1600s, Europeans began wearing hats and clothes made of beaver skins. To supply them, more and

The red-headed woodpecker (below) uses its beak to scoop insects out of trees. It also stores nuts and corn for the winter.

In the Cache River State Natural Area in southern Illinois, bald cypress trees (above) grow in water. Bald cypress are rare in the Midwest, and usually only grow in the South.

more trappers looked for beavers in the American wilderness. Trapping beavers became such a big business that the animals were wiped out in some places. Beavers probably vanished from Illinois by 1850. Many beavers were reintroduced to Illinois in the 1930s. Protection efforts since then have increased the number of beavers in the state.

Beavers are one of the most important **wetland** animals. In fact, they help create wetlands. They gather twigs and cut down small trees with their powerful teeth. They use these twigs and logs to build **dams** across rivers. These dams turn rivers into ponds filled with plant life.

Almost half of the plants native to Illinois live in wetlands. Bald cypress trees grow in water in Illinois **swamps.** Tupelo gum trees provide fruit for squirrels to eat. Cattails are plants that grow in **marshes.** Native Americans made woven baskets with them. Illinois settlers in the 1800s made a kind of coffee with chicory root gathered in wetlands. Lotus plants grow on water, with round, green leaves shaped like a cup. Creeping water primrose grows in shallow ponds. It has red stems and bright yellow flowers that grow along the water's surface.

One of the easiest plants to find in wetlands is the purple loosestrife. It has purple, spike-shaped flowers. Purple loosestrife takes root in wetlands and spreads quickly. In fact, so much purple loosestrife grows in Illinois wetlands that it crowds out other plants. To stop its spread, the state has made it illegal to sell the plant in Illinois.

Purple loosestrife (above) is actually native to Europe, Russia, and Asia, but it has made its way to the U.S. It spreads quickly in Illinois wetlands and is a threat to the native plants.

Birds are also easy to find in wetlands. Great blue herons stand on their long, skinny legs in shallow water looking for fish. Pied-billed grebes dive underwater looking for fish. When one of these birds senses danger, it will slowly sink under the water. Then it will return to the surface of the pond far from where it went under. One million **waterfowl** visit marshes and swamps each year, as they fly to and from their winter homes.

*Dragonflies (right) feed on mosquitoes in wetlands. As the dragonfly flies through the air, it holds its legs together to form a basket in which it captures insects. The dragonfly grabs hold of its **prey** with its legs or jaws, and may eat it while flying.*

Swimming animals such as muskrats, minks, and raccoons live in **wetlands.** So do many insects. Dragonflies feed on mosquitoes that live in wet areas. Eastern box turtles live in **marshes.** They get their name from their shells, which they close tightly like a box. The Eastern box turtle can pull its head, legs, and tail inside its shell to protect them from **predators** such as raccoons and skunks. Native Americans used the shells of Eastern box turtles as bowls.

Muskrats

Muskrats (left) can hold their breath underwater for ten to fifteen minutes at a time. That comes in handy when they are building their lodges in the water. Their lodges are made of cattails, twigs, and mud. Muskrats are known to be big eaters. They mostly eat wetland plants, like cattails. In the winter, they chew holes in ice to get at plants under the water.

RIVER LIFE

The rivers that wind through Illinois make a home for plants and animals in the water and on land. Near their shores, cottonwood trees grow. Their buds provide food for grouse, a kind of bird. Thousands of mayflies swarm over rivers in the early evening. Bullfrogs try to catch them, or other insects, for dinner. In the winter, the bullfrogs bury themselves in soft mud to **hibernate.**

Bald eagles soar over Illinois rivers, looking for fish. When they spot one, they swoop down at 50 miles per hour (80 kilometers per hour) and catch their prey with their sharp **talons.** Wood ducks perch in trees, eating seeds. Belted kingfishers dive for fish in quiet streams.

Illinois's state fish is the bluegill. Bluegills weigh only about a pound (0.5 kilograms), but people who like to fish

Bullfrogs (below) catch insects on Illinois rivers. The bullfrog is the largest frog of the United States. Bullfrogs grow to be about 8 inches (20 centimeters) long, not including their hind legs.

River Otters

The river otter (right) is an animal made for the water. Its thick fur protects it from cold. Its long body and short, powerful legs help it glide easily through the water. River otters are easy to spot. They can only hold their breath for a few minutes at a time, so they have to come to the surface often. In the 1800s, hunters collecting otter furs killed so many otters that they nearly vanished from Illinois. In 1990, only about 100 survived in the state. They could only be found in the northwest corner of the state, on the Mississippi River. Today, the number of river otters in Illinois is increasing due to the protection efforts of environmental groups.

know that they are terrific fighters. Largemouth bass, catfish, and rainbow darters are some of the other types of fish often found in rivers in Illinois. The rainbow darter is named for the bright stripes of color on its back and fins. It lives on the rocky bottom of clear streams and feeds on insects, snails, and crayfish. Three hundred types of fish swim in Illinois rivers.

The rainbow darter (below) is named for the bright colors on its back and fins. Rainbow darters live in creeks and rivers all over Illinois.

LAKE LIFE

Deep under the water of Illinois, crabs crawl across lake floors. Tiny plant-like creatures called **algae** float in the water and provide food for shrimp and small fish. Algae sometimes look like a green carpet floating on the water. Many kinds of larger fish swim in Illinois lakes. Largemouth bass, tiger muskies, rainbow trout, and perch are favorites of anglers. Lake sturgeon swim along the floors of lakes and suck up snails, clams, and crayfish with their scoop-like mouths. One of the most beautiful fish found in Illinois is the longear sunfish, with its brightly colored skin. It follows turtles around as they feed on lake bottoms. The sunfish scoops up the insect eggs and other food that the turtle's movement stirs up.

Birds make their homes near lakes, as well. Ospreys, terns, and cormorants feed on fish. Cormorants will dive 25 feet (7.6 meters) below the surface of a lake to catch a fish. **Migrating** birds rest on shore as they make their way from their winter homes in the south to their summer homes in the north. More than 100,000 Canada geese spend their winters at Horseshoe Lake in southern Illinois.

Fish that live in Lake Michigan have to compete with alien **species.** An alien species is one that comes from another place to make a new home. The alewife is an alien species of fish that now lives in Lake Michigan. Alewives can live in both saltwater and freshwater. They are a kind of herring native to the Atlantic Ocean. They came to Lake Michigan in the 1930s, probably in the hulls of ships. When those ships docked in Lake Michigan, the alewives escaped. By the 1960s, so many alewives

Canada geese (below) rest in Illinois lakes during their long migrations. Hundreds of thousands of Canada geese spend their winters on lakes in southern Illinois.

Zebra Mussels

The zebra mussel (right) is a kind of shelled animal that lives in water. Zebra mussels are native to Europe. However, in the 1980s, they came to Lake Michigan in the water tanks of boats. Once released in the lake, they spread rapidly. Zebra mussels have no natural predators in the lake. Tens of millions live in Lake Michigan. They eat so much **algae** and other plant life that little food is left for other animals. They also clog water pipes. Zebra mussels are now spreading to other lakes in Illinois.

lived in Lake Michigan that they were crowding out other animals. **Conservation** officials introduced coho salmon to Lake Michigan. The coho salmon feed on alewives and keep them from taking over the lake.

CITIES, SUBURBS, AND FARMS

Cities, **suburbs,** and farms are created by humans, but wild plants and animals can find homes there, too. Small patches of prairie still survive in a few places in the Chicago area. So do small **marshes.** Herons fish in the Calumet River, not far from steel mills and factories. Peregrine falcons nest on a few tall buildings in downtown Chicago. These birds hunt for mice, rabbits, and smaller birds. They can fly 200 miles per hour (320 kilometers per hour) when they are hunting.

Some animals find homes in the parks, gardens, and golf courses of cities and suburbs. Cottontail rabbits eat garden plants without fear of attack by **predators** like owls or foxes. Without predators, the number of rabbits in a garden can grow so quickly that the garden can't survive. Bright red cardinals feed on seeds and insects in backyards. Chipmunks leave trails of nut shells behind as they wander through leafy suburbs.

The ailanthus, or tree of heaven, grows in city parks and in cracks of sidewalks. The ailanthus came from Asia to California in the 1850s. Its seeds spread on the wind and now the tree lives all over the United States. It is well-suited to the city. It doesn't need much room, and air pollution doesn't bother it.

Driving down a highway lined with farms, it is easy to spot red-winged blackbirds. These birds usually make their homes in **wetlands,** but they also like farms with ponds. Quail and pheasant nest on farms, too. Pheasant can be seen on roadsides eating small pebbles, which help them digest their food. Bluebirds feed on seeds, berries, and grasshoppers that they find in orchards. A bluebird's eyesight is so good that it can spot a grasshopper 100 feet (30.5 meters) away.

Coyotes

Coyotes (left) look a little like German shepherd dogs, but they carry their tails lower than dogs. They also have their own kind of howl, which can be heard for miles. They live all over Illinois, even in cities and suburbs. As suburbs grow, land that used to be coyote **habitat** is turned into backyards. As a result, coyotes may come in contact with humans and their pets. Coyotes usually eat rabbits, mice, and other small animals. However, they have been known to attack small pet dogs in backyards. Coyotes have even wandered into downtown Chicago looking for food.

Then and Now

Just 200 years ago, Illinois looked much different than it does today. Forests and prairies stood where our cities and **suburbs** stand today. **Bison,** elk, wolves, and even mountain lions walked on paths that are now highways. Huge flocks of birds flew where our airplanes fly today.

Illinois changed forever when large numbers of settlers moved there in the 1800s. They cleared the forests for wood. They turned the prairies into productive farms. It is now impossible to return to the days of huge forests and vast prairies. However, it is possible to protect the plants and animals that still live in Illinois.

Chicago-area forest preserves date back to 1915. Although many trees have been cut down, there are still woodlands around Illinois. This is part of the Caldwell Woods (below) in Niles, Illinois.

Bison

French explorers Jacques Marquette and Louis Jolliet traveled through Illinois in 1673. They wrote of "wild cattle" that could be seen grazing in the prairies. They were describing bison (left). Bison were the largest animals that lived in the prairies. They fed on the grasses and flowering plants there. Bison disappeared not long after settlers moved to Illinois in the 1800s. Hunters killed off many bison. Also, as the prairies were turned into farms, bison lost their **habitat.** Today, they live only in nature preserves like the one at Fermi National Laboratory in Batavia.

PROTECTING WILDLIFE

By 1900, many plants and animals of Illinois were disappearing. Bison were nearly killed off by hunters. Passenger pigeons were on their way to **extinction.** Something had to be done to protect wildlife and their homes. In the early 1900s, people in Illinois and across the country began protecting natural places.

In 1915, Cook and DuPage Counties set up the state's first forest preserves. Their goal was to protect wildlife for the "education, pleasure and recreation of the public." The counties bought large pieces of land and made it possible for plants and animals to live there unharmed.

In 1924, the United States government established the Upper Mississippi River National Wildlife and Fish Refuge. A wildlife **refuge** is a natural area where animals can find the shelter, food, and water they need to survive. The Upper Mississippi River National Wildlife and Fish Refuge is home to many of Illinois's bald eagles. The Cypress Creek National Wildlife Refuge in southern Illinois provides a home for 50 **species** of **threatened** and **endangered** plants and animals. Its bald cypress trees are among the oldest living things in North America.

Illinois Wildlife Refuges

Today, there are several national wildlife refuges in Illinois. They help to protect the plants and animals of the state.

Some are more than 1,000 years old. Today, there are several national wildlife **refuges** in Illinois.

In 1938, the U.S. government opened the Shawnee National Forest in southern Illinois. It is Illinois's only national forest and covers 277,000 acres (112,098 hectares). Visitors there can see what Illinois's oak and hickory forests may have looked like 200 years ago.

Laws helped protect plants and animals, too. The Clean Water Act of 1972 helped make lakes and rivers cleaner.

That made them safer for the plants and animals that live in and near them.

In 1973, the Illinois Department of Conservation began listing **threatened** and **endangered species.** By law, plants and animals on these lists were protected from harm. The lists also helped educate people about threats to the survival of plants and animals.

Shawnee National Forest (above) was founded in 1938. It is Illinois's only national forest. It covers 277,000 acres (112,098 hectares) and is home to a huge variety of plant and animal species.

NEW HOMES FOR PLANTS AND ANIMALS

In the 1960s, people began working to bring prairies back to parts of Illinois. This effort is called prairie **restoration.** Restoring a prairie takes years. First, seeds of prairie grasses and wildflowers must be planted. Then plants that don't belong in prairies must be weeded out. Workers sometimes use controlled fires to help make the soil rich. The ashes of the plants put nutrients back into the soil.

One of the first prairie restorations in Illinois was started at Lisle's Morton Arboretum in 1962. Fermi National

Laboratory in Batavia began a prairie restoration in 1972. The small prairie there is even home to several **bison.** One of the largest prairie restorations is the Midewin National Tallgrass Prairie near Joliet. It covers 15,000 acres (6,070 hectares) where an arms plant of the U.S. Army once stood. The prairie is home to five plant **species** that are **threatened** or **endangered** in the U.S.: Mead's milkweed, leafy prairie clover, lakeside daisy, prairie bush clover, and the white-fringed orchid.

Since 1975, volunteers have been working to restore the land around Fermilab (above) to the native tallgrass prairie that was once there.

Workers in forest preserves use similar methods to maintain forests. They remove invading species like buckthorn, a weedy tree that crowds out other trees. They clear away dead branches to let more light reach the forest floor. They even plant seeds of native forest plants and trees that no longer live in the area.

RETURNING ANIMALS

White-tailed deer were driven out of Illinois in the 1800s. They were killed in large numbers by hunters. Their forest **habitats** were cut down. By 1912, the animals no longer lived in Illinois. However, in 1933, the Department of Conservation brought white-tailed deer from other places to live in Illinois again. This process is called reintroducing a species. Today, the white-tailed deer can be found in large numbers all over the state. It is actually the state animal of Illinois.

Other animals have been reintroduced to Illinois. Sand-hill cranes are large, gray birds that live in **marshes** and other **wetlands.** In the 1800s, many of their nesting sites were destroyed to build towns. They disappeared from Illinois by around 1870. However, efforts to restore cranes' natural habitat have been successful. Today, cranes are nesting again in northern Illinois.

Trappers killed off large numbers of river otters in the late 1800s and early 1900s. By 1990, only about 100 river otters survived in Illinois. However, more river otters were reintroduced to Illinois in 1995. Eighty-one otters from Louisiana were brought to Illinois and released in rivers. Today, they can be found all over the state.

Much has changed in Illinois. Species have been killed off or driven out of the state. Entire forests have been cut down. Even rivers have been made to change their course. Still, Illinois remains full of plants and animals that can teach us about the natural world. They are found in cities, **suburbs,** farms, forests, rivers, and lakes. Wherever they are, they are certainly worth protecting, now and in the future.

The white-tailed deer (left) has made a comeback in Illinois. It is the largest mammal living in the state and one of the fastest. It can run up to 35 miles (56 kilometers) per hour. It is also the state animal of Illinois.

Glossary

adaptation feature of a plant or animal that helps it survive in its home

algae group of simple plants that have no leaves, stems, or roots and grow in water or on wet surfaces

ancestor plant or animal of the past from which today's species have developed

aquatic having to do with water

bison also sometimes called a buffalo; large, shaggy-maned mammal with short horns and a hump

bog area of soft, wet earth and decayed vegetation

climate weather conditions that are typical of a place

conservation effort to preserve natural resources such as soil, water, and forest from pollution and destruction

dam wall built through a river to stop water flow; to stop the flow of water by building a dam

decay rot or fall apart

dredge scoop or dig up earth from the bottom of a river or lake

ecosystem community of living things, together with the environment in which they live

endangered put at risk or in danger

extinct no longer living

extirpated no longer living in a certain place, having moved to another

fawn young deer

fertile rich, productive

filter something that screens out dangerous or harmful substances

fossil remains or traces of a living thing of long ago

girdling killing trees by cutting away rings of bark from their trunks

glacier large sheet of ice that spreads very slowly over land

grove small wooded area

habitat natural home of a plant or animal

herb flowering plant valued for its flavor or scent

hibernate spend the winter keeping still in a safe place to save energy

mammoth large, extinct animal, similar to an elephant, with shaggy hair and long tusks

marsh wet, low-lying area, often thick with tall grasses

mastodon large, extinct animal, similar to an elephant, with tusks and shaggy hair. Mastodons usually lived in forests.

migrate move from one place to another on a regular schedule; migration is the act of migrating

mineral solid substance formed in the earth by nature and obtained by mining

missionary person sent by a church to spread his or her religious beliefs; a mission is a place where missionaries live and work

pasture ground covered with grass for horses, cattle, or other animals to feed on

predator animal that eats another animal

prey animal hunted for food by another animal

reed stalk of a tall grass found in wet places

refuge safe place

resource valuable thing that can be made useful; there are natural and manmade resources

restoration process of renewing or rebuilding

saber-toothed cat extinct animal named for its long, sharp upper teeth

sediment dirt and other solid material that settles at the bottom of rivers and lakes

skyscraper very tall building

species group of living things that resemble one another, have common ancestors, and can breed with one another

stockyard place where hogs, cattle, and other animals are kept

suburb city or town just outside a larger city; suburban means having to do with a suburb

swamp wet, low-lying area with trees growing in shallow water

talon claw of a bird

threatened facing possible coming danger

urban of or having to do with cities

waterfowl birds such as geese or ducks that live on or near water

wetlands very wet, low-lying land

More Books to Read

DuTemple, Lesley A. *North American Cranes.* Minneapolis, Minn.: Lerner Publishing, 1999.

Feeley, Kathleen. *Illinois: The Prairie State.* Milwaukee, Wis.: Gareth Stevens, 2002.

Fink Martin, Patricia A. *Prairies, Fields, and Meadows.* Danbury, Conn.: Franklin Watts, 2002.

Frisch, Aaron. *Deer.* North Mankato, Minn.: Smart Apple Media, 2000.

Green, Jen. *Butterflies.* Tarrytown, N.Y.: Marshall Cavendish, 1999.

Hodgkins, Fran. *Animals among Us: Living with Suburban Wildlife.* North Haven, Conn.: Shoe String Press, 2000.

Priebe, Mac. *The Peregrine Falcon: Endangered No More.* Norwalk, Conn.: Mindfull Publishing, 1999.

Robbins, Ken. *Thunder on the Plains: The Story of the American Buffalo.* New York: Atheneum Books, 2001.

Williams, Kimberly Joan and Erik Daniel Stoops. *Bat Conservation.* Benton Harbor, Mich.: Faulkner's, 2001.

Index

About the Author

Andrew Santella lives in Trout Valley, Illinois, and is a lifelong resident of the state of Illinois. He is the author of 25 nonfiction books for children. He also writes for publications such as *GQ* and the *New York Times Book Review*.